# WARWICK'S

# FAMOUS SON

# The Story of Thomas Oken

# and his Charity

*Oken's House as it may have appeared in his day*
(Grahame Ward)

# WARWICK'S MOST FAMOUS SON

## The Story of Thomas Oken and his Charity

## Paul Bolitho

The Charity of Thomas Oken and Nicholas Eyffler

First published by
The Charity of Thomas Oken and Nicholas Eyffler
May 2003

ISBN  0  9545276  0  7

A Cataloguing in Publication Record
for this title is available from the British Library.

Typeset in Baskerville Old Face
Printed in Great Britain by
Warwick Printing Company Limited

# Contents

# List of Illustrations

In memory of

HERBERT WALDEN, C.B.E.,

trustee, friend and elder statesman

# *Preface*

I am grateful for being given the opportunity by the Trustees to write this history of the Charity founded by Warwick's greatest son. I acknowledge with thanks the help given me in advice and access to documents by Mr. Herbert Walden and Mr. Ralph Thornton, two of the Trustees, and Mr. Terence Horn, the former Clerk and Receiver to the Trustees. His Secretary, Mrs. Jill Betts, kindly introduced me to several of the residents of both the Castle Hill and Bowling Green Street properties, and they were all very happy to give me their impressions of living there. I am grateful to Mr. Grahame Ward and Mr. Roger Wilson for providing the photographs. With help from Mr Jerry Weber and other members of the staff I have also made extensive use of the Charity's archives deposited at the County Record Office, and Mr. Derek Maudlin, the Town Clerk, also gave assistance. And a big thank you to my wife Doreen as well for her understanding whilst I have been so often incommunicado on this venture. The Trustees and I are also grateful for the grant from the Trustees of King Henry VIII Charity towards the cost of publication.

My aim has been to write a narrative history of the Trust which will be of interest to the general public, and especially to Warwickians past and present. Whilst at all times seeking to be accurate, it does not pretend to be an academic treatise. As it is intended for the general reader, I have dispensed with extensive footnotes, but quoted where necessary in the text and included a bibliography of sources. When quoting I have modernised spellings, and, for example, often used the more familiar word 'Trustees' when in earlier times I should have used the word 'Feoffees'.

My task has been made easier by the transcriptions of others: by Thomas Kemp's transcription of the Black Book of Warwick, Michael Farr's of college and corporation accounts, the records of Nicholas Eyffler and the Great Fire of Warwick, and especially by George Tibbits' transcription and history of the Charity's records themselves.

Finally with whatever help I have had comes the usual disclaimer: any errors which may have inadvertently crept in are mine and mine alone.

Paul Bolitho
17 Oken Court,
Warwick

*Brass rubbing of Thomas Oken and his wife Joan from his memorial in St. Mary's (Ralph Thornton)*

# —1—

# *Introduction*

Warwick in the sixteenth century was still a small town of about 2500 inhabitants dominated by the Castle and St. Mary's Church. It was laid out in a cross pattern of two main roads stretching from East Gate to West Gate, and from North Gate (no longer standing in Tudor times) to the Castle commanding the southern approaches to the town. There was a wall ditch along the line of the present Barrack Street and another dyke still in existence between the Castle and West Gate, but otherwise most of the mediaeval fortifications of the town had crumbled away, and suburbs had sprung up in Smith Street, Mill Street and Bridge End, West Street and the Saltisford. Though the feudal power of the Earls of Warwick was on the wane, they still exerted considerable influence: for example, several of the market days owed their existence to their charters, and the Earl of Warwick was also Recorder of Warwick, responsible for law and order. The lives of the citizens were also governed to a large extent by the Church, and the magnificent addition of the Beauchamp Chapel of Our Lady in the previous century reminded them of their allegiance both to the spiritual and the temporal powers. Not that they necessarily felt oppressed: the influence of the members of the united craft Guild was considerable, and they were in process of being transformed into a Town Council. The Guild of St. George and the Guild of the Holy Trinity and the Blessed Virgin had been founded in 1383, serving social and religious as well as commercial purposes. By 1415 they had amalgamated under the name of the Guild of the Holy Trinity and St. George and met in the buildings we know as the Lord Leycester Hospital which had been erected by Thomas Beauchamp II, Earl of Warwick, towards the end of the fourteenth century.

This was the town in which Warwick's greatest son lived. Unfortunately very little is known about the life of Thomas Oken and no portrait of him exists He died in 1573, fifteen years into the reign of Elizabeth I, but we do not know his exact date of birth. Assuming, however, that he was born shortly before the death of Henry VII in 1509, his life spanned the reigns of all five Tudor monarchs, or six if we include,

*The Guild of the Holy Trinity and St. George (now the Lord Leycester Hospital)*

as we must, Lady Jane Grey, the tragic 'Nine Days' Queen', whose father-in-law, the Earl of Warwick who became Duke of Northumberland, sought to put upon the throne.

In our computer age of rapid change, we tend in retrospect to think of the Tudor Age as a whole, one year much the same as another, a period of relative stability and marking time after the upsets of the Wars of the Roses. To those who lived at the time nothing could be farther from the truth: the changes they experienced were far more drastic in their eyes than those which we take in our stride today. The anti-Papal policy of Henry VIII, the lurch towards Protestantism under Edward VI, the Catholic reaction under Mary and finally the Anglican settlement under Elizabeth were enough to disturb profoundly any Englishman, but the political implications of this religious revolution were far more cataclysmic. It is a tribute to the acumen of a man as conservative as Thomas Oken who loved the old order of things that he was prepared regretfully to accept that the time-honoured institutions of mediaeval Guild and Collegiate Church with dean and chapter had to go, and that he was equally prepared to enter uncharted waters and adapt the new means at his disposal for the future good of the town. It was an age when the least disapproval of The Powers That Be, of whatever hue, courted martyrdom. But martyrs, though they keep the faith, do not solve the problems; only 'statesmen' like Thomas Oken, who put aside their feelings of outrage in order to get the best deal they can for their fellow men, establish a secure future for them. And without Oken's astute negotiations with the King's commissioners there would be no (grossly misnamed) King Henry VIII Charity today.

*The old Guildhall at the Lord Leycester Hospital (Walter Scott, Bradford)*

# — 2 —

# *Thomas Oken*

Thomas Oken was born in Warwick in humble circumstances, although, as I say, we do not know his date of birth. He amassed a considerable fortune as a mercer, a textile merchant dealing especially in silks and other costly materials, and when he died childless (his wife Joan pre-deceased him) he was to leave all his wealth to charity. He lived in and carried on his business from the gabled half-timbered house in Castle Street which is still owned by Oken's Charity and is now the Dolls' Museum. It stood on the main north-south thoroughfare of the town which ran past the parish church and down round the castle boundary walls (then much closer to the Castle itself) to the old bridge over the river. A short distance away was the Cross marking the junction of that road with the other main street running east-west.

Few references to Oken's financial dealings now exist. Those that do make no mention of fine silks, but rather show that like many another successful entrepreneur he diversified his business interests and was not too proud to sell more mundane items. For example, in 1552 the Corporation paid him 1s. for two skins of parchment with which to make their account book, and in 1565 1d. for some cord with which to mend the bellows of St. Mary's organ. Much earlier in 1537 he had provided the old Collegiate body with a hundred pounds of beeswax for 6s., a considerable sum of money in those days.

However, we know more about Oken the citizen than about Oken the mercer, and it was as a citizen that his finest hour came at a time of crisis for the town. In September 1544 he became Master of the town's united craft Guild of the Holy Trinity and St. George – before its buildings were acquired by the Earl of Leicester for his Hospital., but at a time when Henry VIII was following up his dissolution of the monasteries with further depredations of church and guild property. The immediate visible effect of the Chantries Act of 1545 for the townspeople would have been the abolition of the three chantry priests in the Chapel of Our Lady in St. Mary's who were required to say daily masses for the soul of Richard Beauchamp for ever. But it was the property of the Church and the Guild acquired by the King which was of more importance to the leading townsfolk, property which the King's commissioners were somehow

*St. Mary's Church as it was in Oken's day*

persuaded to restore to the town under the guise of the misnamed King Henry VIII Charity.

In fact, knowing that its property would be confiscated anyway under the forthcoming Chantries Act (now more correctly called the Dissolution of Colleges Act), St. Mary's Church voluntarily surrendered that property and its collegiate status to the Crown some time between April and July 1544. In addition to this, the Guild was also under threat of abolition by the Crown. However, tough negotiations with the King's Commissioners resulted in the resettlement upon the people of Warwick of a substantial part of the Church and Guild endowments, and, as George Tibbits convincingly argues, it was Thomas Oken as Master of the Guild who led these negotiations. May 15th 1545 was a red-letter day for the town. On that day the King Henry VIII Charity was set up by Letters Patent and endowed with much of the property previously owned by the Church, and a month later the Guild also transferred its Guildhall property to the Charity, in so doing saving those estates for the town as well. Also on May 15th the town received a Charter which the Guild had been able to purchase from the King for £39. 13s. 4d. through the sale of a little of its land. This Charter established a Corporation of burgesses to manage the properties, and continuity was maintained because the members of the Guild became the first burgesses, and the Guild itself was not abolished until Easter 1548*. Indeed until the nineteenth century town councillors

---

* Not 1546. Tibbits found that the Common Council of the Guild and the Common Council of the Corporation were one and the same for three years, not one, as is commonly supposed.

*Thomas Oken heads the List of Warwick's Leading Citizens*

and King Henry VIII Charity Trustees – and indeed the Trustees of Oken's Charity – were one and the same body of people, administering the funds of all three somewhat indiscriminately.

Thomas Oken was in all likelihood Warwick's very first Bailiff, or, strictly, Principal Burgess, as the Mayor was then called. Although the Corporation records only start at Michaelmas 1545 with Richard Fisher as Bailiff, Tibbits argues that it seems probable that Oken's term of office which began as Master of the Guild at Michaelmas 1544 ended as Bailiff a year later because the members of the Guild became the first burgesses by the Charter part way through the year.

When Henry VIII died in 1547 his nine year old son became king as Edward VI, and the pace of change quickened, first under the Duke of Somerset as Lord Protector and then under John Dudley, Earl of Warwick and Duke of Northumberland, who, although he did not take the title of Protector, was at the head of the Council of Regency. But when the sickly Edward died in 1553, the Crown passed to his Catholic half-sister Mary, and the Duke of Northumberland vainly sought to maintain his Protestant power base by proclaiming Lady Jane Grey, the wife of his son Lord Guildford Dudley, as Queen in London. It is not impossible that as Earl of Warwick the Duke could also have had her proclaimed as Queen in Warwick, because we have a lease of property in the town belonging to Oken himself dated "the 20th of July, 1st year of Jane, 1553". If so, with Northumberland, the tragic Lady Jane and her husband executed and two more of Northumberland's sons (the future Earls of Warwick and Leicester) imprisoned, Oken and the other burgesses, as loyal servants of their liege lord, may have found themselves in some personal danger from the Catholic backlash. Nevertheless, they must have weathered any storm because Queen Mary granted the town a further Charter on November 12th, 1554, granting the corporation extra revenues from market tolls and full incorporation for general municipal purposes not granted in the 1545 Charter, and Oken himself became Bailiff a second time from 1557 to 1558 in the final year of Mary's reign.

By mid-life Oken was a wealthy man, generous with his money, and, for those days, widely travelled and connected. How otherwise could he have gained the considerable knowledge of intended legislation necessary to negotiate effectively with the King's Commissioners? Mention of legacies to Stratford and Banbury in his will show that he was well connected there, and since Shakespeare's father was a dealer in wool we can assume they must have known each other. More importantly Oken must have had considerable business relations with mercers and others in Coventry which was an important commercial centre at the time, particularly in the cloth trade. He gave £13. 6s. 8d. to the Carthusian Convent of St. Anne there because in September 1539 the Prior of that house granted an annual pension of £1. 6s. "to our beloved and faithful Thomas Oken for his good and laudable services to us before this time given, and in consideration of 20 marks to us for the use of the aforesaid house given and paid when our said house was formally redeemed from the King, and other great benefits to the said house in divers ways." And in

*The Author as Thomas Oken on St. Mary's 'Living History' Day (Alan Griffin)*

*A Declaration of constitutions, ordinances and decrees of the mysteries and craftsof mercers, haberdashers, grocers and fishmongers within the Borough of Warwick, 1574*
*(Warwickshire County Record Office CR1618/W3/1)*

August 1564 Oken granted to the Cappers Company of Coventry "a house in a street sometime called Gosford Street, now the Jordan Well", the rents and profits from which were to be distributed among the poor of that trade. He also wanted the Cappers to hold an annual service in St. Michael's Church and gave them 2s. a year for their own feast (for "recreation and refreshing"). Farther afield still, Oken is known to have had connections with Buckingham and Reading, though, surprisingly, there is no record of him having had any dealings with the great livery Company of Mercers in the City of London.

No doubt Thomas Oken welcomed the rather more settled years following the accession of Queen Elizabeth. In 1570 he made his will, and a few weeks later two deeds disposing of his property: by now a widower, he was to leave all his wealth for the good of the town. One wonders – Did he consciously establish his own charity because he thought there was always the possibility that the Crown could repossess King Henry VIII funds? Perhaps not Good Queen Bess herself, but the Pope had just excommunicated her and absolved her subjects from their allegiance to her. And then there was the Earl of Leicester on the prowl.

Oken and his fellow burgesses had continued to use the old Guildhall premises for Corporation purposes – until in 1571, with permission from the Queen to secure premises in either Warwick or Kenilworth, Leicester demanded the buildings for his Hospital for old soldiers. The Corporation gave way, presumably because Leicester threatened to take his prestigious scheme to Kenilworth if they did not agree: the burgesses did indeed ask for and eventually receive alternative accommodation (St. Peter's Chapel over the East Gate, the Shire Hall and the Cross Tavern where the Court House now stands), but they are all said to have signed the letter offering Leicester the buildings, Oken presumably included – after all you didn't disagree with a man as powerful as the Earl of Leicester who was also the brother of the Earl of Warwick. However, Thomas Oken, now a father figure in the town, dared to point out that they were ill-advised to give away such useful buildings – and he got away with his temerity.

We know this because John Fisher considered a speech of Oken's in the Common Council on November 4th 1571 (the only speech of his we have) as worthy of reporting at length in 'The Black Book of Warwick'. Oken referred to the Corporation as being "a thing most precious to be esteemed, being obtained not only by great industry and labour of our predecessors but also with no small charges and expense" – presumably a reference to his own efforts a quarter of a century before to obtain the Charter from Henry VIII. He went on to call to mind "what good and profitable things the King had bestowed which now being in our possession are not so husbandly handled as he thinketh they might, namely for this cause that we are so readily bent to grant for little or nothing things of good value". He obviously regretted that his beloved Guildhall which he had reclaimed for a Town Hall back in 1545 should be made over to the Earl for other purposes after so short a time. He could, however, console himself with the thought that he had just established his own charity for the town.

As one of the principal burgesses he would have been present at Leicester's celebration of the Feast of St. Michael in St. Mary's on Michaelmas Day in 1571 and at the funeral there of the Marquis of Northampton in December that year. And if his health had permitted he would have gone forth with the Bailiff to meet Queen Elizabeth when she visited Warwick in August 1572. By that time he would have been living quietly in retirement: we are told that there were few wares in his shop at the time of his death, and whilst he died rich in terms of property and money, we shall find no mention of goods in either his will or the deed establishing his charity.

Thomas Oken died at his house in Castle Street on July 29th or, possibly, July 30th* 1573 and his funeral took place at St. Mary's on August 4th.

He probably died a disappointed man. His dreams appeared to have been shattered: his Guldhall had been taken away from him a couple of years previously, and the Earl of Leicester did not fulfil his side of the bargain and provide the burgesses with the alternative buildings which

---

* Thomas Kemp in his notes on the "Black Book", p. 169, quotes an old minute book, presumably the Warwick Borough Record of 1612 (CR1618/W21/6).

they asked for until two years after Oken's death. But we know that with hindsight he had absolutely no reason to feel depressed. He has left three great institutions to posterity – the King Henry VIII Charity which we have already mentioned and Oken's Charity and Warwick School to which we shall refer later.

In passing, we may note that there is an extant document of 1574 in the County Record Office entitled "Declaration of constitutions, ordinances and decrees of the mysteries and crafts of mercers, haberdashers, grocers and fishmongers within the Borough of Warwick", a sure indication of the importance of Oken's trade in the area. We may wonder at the conjunction of mercers and fishmongers, but it connects Oken with that other important self-made Warwick family of Elizabethan times: John Fisher of the "Black Book" and Thomas Fisher who rebuilt the Priory, the sons of a Mr. Hawkins who became known as Fisher because he sold fish in the Market Place.

Incidentally, why has no portrait of Thomas Oken come down to us when we have one of his friend Nicholas Eyffler? He could certainly have afforded to have one painted. Perhaps one disappeared in the course of time. Or perhaps one never existed. Could it be that Oken refused to sit for his portrait, that, despite his prominence in the life of the town, he was a very modest sort of person?

# — 3 —

# *Oken's Death*

As much appears to be known about Thomas Oken's dying as his living because of an unseemly dispute over his will before he was actually dead! It has come down to us because one of the participants in the drama, John Fisher, recorded it in detail in 'The Black Book of Warwick'. There were actually two wills or copies of the will, both dated the same day in November 1570. Both wills were substantially the same, but one contained a few extra bequests for the town. And no gift of any residue was mentioned. A recipe for disaster! Perhaps Oken himself expected some trouble because in addition to appointing Robert Phillips and Thomas Cawdrey as his executors, he also named half a dozen 'overseers' to look after the executors! In the event Fisher implies that the executors and their wives were hoping to profit from the shorter document.

The day before he died in July 1573 Oken was asked by Ralph Griffin, a clergyman and the first Master of the Lord Leycester Hospital, and Thomas Powell, one of the overseers, which version of the will stood and he indicated the one which contained the extra legacies. However, Powell was not satisfied that Oken's wishes would be carried out and asked the Town Clerk, John Fisher, a fellow overseer, to go with him to call on Oken who was, however, very ill, and asked them to come back another time. A little later Powell and Fisher paid another visit to the house along with Thomas Jenks, the Bailiff, and William Frekenton, a third overseer. They were met at the door by Griffin who told them that Oken could no longer speak. However, desirous of obtaining a copy of the will, the overseers went indoors to confront Cawdrey, Mrs. Cawdrey and Mrs. Phillips (Phillips was away in London) who were there with others waiting for Oken to expire!

After some discussion the wills were produced, read, differences noted, countersigned and sealed. Fisher then returned one copy to Mrs. Phillips and passed the other to the Bailiff for safe keeping, Cawdrey in a rage trying to snatch the Bailiff's copy and only succeeding in tearing a bit out! "This troubled so much the unreasonable women", we are told, "that they sticked not to say that if Mr. Oken did ever speak again the town should have not one groat of his goods nor land neither if they could help it. And therewith went into the chamber where the man lay in extreme passions and there cried out, rubbed him using all the means they could devise to torment him and so to make him speak if it were possible using such outcries and screeches that not only all the house was troubled and disquieted but also a great part of the neighbours in the street wondered to hear them."

However, the Bailiff and his colleagues refused to give way and came away with the longer version of the will in their possession. In such circumstances Thomas Oken breathed his last. And before the poor man was buried, the quarrel between executors and overseers flared up again. Phillips (back from London) and Cawdrey locked themselves in one of the rooms to go through the chests containing money and plate, and when the overseers arrived only opened up when Fisher threatened to break down the door! We only have the one side of the story (of which Tibbits himself is sceptical): Fisher in the Black Book implies that Phillips and Cawdrey were helping themselves and only opened up when they had had time to "shuffle up all their gear" and return it to the chests. On the other hand, despite the protestations of Oken's housekeeper Agnes Catur that "my master's mind was that there should be no one chest opened until all his overseers were present as well as you", the executors may well have thought that they had full authority and it was no business of the overseers, and so then determined to be as awkward as possible! Whatever the rights and wrongs of the protagonists, there turned out to be a great deal of money at stake!

After much talk the executors agreed to prove the will by Michaelmas and pay all the legacies before the following Spring, and the overseers eventually left the house at 2am! Phillips and Cawdrey then continued sorting through the plate and money until daybreak!

However, the executors were in no hurry to proceed. Eventually some of the beneficiaries began to complain to the overseers, and the Corporation demanded the plate and £100 left to them. Having had no joy from Phillips and Cawdrey by the following Easter, Fisher went to the Court of Arches when he was in London. Here he was shown a copy of the will which actually omitted some of its provisions! As I have indicated, we only have his side of the story, but Fisher was obviously convinced the executors were up to no good. Phillips for his part complained about Fisher's conduct to Sir Thomas Lucy (the man who caught young Will Shakespeare poaching), and he invited the warring parties to dinner at Charlecote in order to arbitrate. Phillips put his case at such length that everybody got fed up, and after Fisher was given the chance to reply, Sir Thomas decided that the overseers had acted correctly, berated Phillips and Cawdrey and ordered them to pay all the legacies, which at long last they agreed to do provided Fisher stopped harassing them.

This story, incidentally, raises certain unanswered queries. In what capacity did Sir Thomas Lucy act? As a justice, though probably not the closest to hand? And could Nicholas Eyffler, Oken's friend, who as we shall see probably did work for Sir Thomas, have acted as an intermediary?

Because this dispute over Oken's will began before he died, we have not yet considered its contents. We examine the various legacies in the next chapter.

# — 4 —

# *Oken's Will*

T he will dated November 24th 1570 begins in a way conventional for the time, but none the less sincerely meant by the pious Thomas Oken: "First and principally I give and bequeath my soul to Almighty God, my only Maker and Redeemer, trusting through the merits of His passion to be saved, and my body to be buried in the parish church of St. Mary in Warwick against St. Anne's altar hard by the wall, and there I will to have a little tomb of stone, and on the said tomb in the stone wall I will to have an epitaph of brass with two pictures, one of myself and the other of my wife, with these words graven under 'Jesu have mercy upon me; Jesu have mercy upon me'. "

After requiring 5s. to be paid in tithes, 'negligently forgotten' (obviously, a stickler for paying up), he details his funeral expenses at length: 2s. for the vicar who conducts the service, 1s. for any other clergyman officiating, 4d. for each choirboy, and 1s. each for the four pallbearers, the eight bellringers and the gravedigger. His housekeeper Agnes Catur is allowed to rent the house for the rest of her life, and gets £10 and a silver goblet "for taking pains for me when I had the ague and the gout." The executors and overseers also benefit financially (the former got £40 each, but the latter only £2, so in the event Phillips and Cawdrey could hardly complain!); a couple of debts are remitted; and all his tenants get let off a quarter's rent. Warwick Corporation gets £100 to buy common land (they duly bought 'St. Michael's Piece' – probably the Pigwells – from Sir John Puckering in 1583), and both Stratford and Banbury get £40 each. Oken also gives £5 for the maintenance of the highways of Warwick and a further £5 towards the building of the Market House. Warwick's burgesses also get three goblets, a salt cellar and eighteen spoons. And his concern for a town of thatched houses is shown by his leaving money to purchase twelve leather fire buckets.

But it is his concern for the poor which shines through. There is 4d. each to pay for dinners for six poor men and six poor women who are to bring his body to the church; they are also to be given some six yards of material each to be made into coats. Three or four days after his burial 300 of the poorest households in Warwick are to receive 1s. each, and in a year's time another 300 families are to receive the same. And specifically,

*Opening part of Thomas Oken's Will, Nov.24th, 1570*
*(Record Office CR1618/WA3/84/1)*

thirty poor girls are to receive 6s. 8d. each (the old mark) when they get married.

The Vicar is also to receive 6s. 8d. for declaring God's word to the people that day, and after the service the executors are to prepare dinner for the Bailiff and burgesses and their wives – the origin of Oken's Sermon and Oken's Feast. Another 6s. 8d. is to go to Ralph Griffin to declare God's word "some other day". Griffin had been at Oken's bedside as he lay dying: presumably he was high in the old man's esteem.

Another point of interest is Oken's Chest. "I will the poor man's chest stand fast by where I shall be buried continually to put in all my books and writings with all such other jewels as shall come to their hands. Also I will that the Bailiff and three of his brethren shall have four locks and four keys, and also four honest men of the four wards, that is to say, in every ward one other four locks and four keys. And I will that my Executors shall appoint some other chest to stand in the place."

There are a great number of small bequests in the will, obviously to personal friends and acquaintances he knew well. 10s. to Thomas Lathbury, £1 to Thomas Sheldon, to Thomas Boyar a doublet, a pair of hose and a leather jerkin... The list goes on, and then "to Nicholas Morrell and Thomas Harris 2s.... *for God's sake only*".

Why this phrase? Canon Julian Rudd* suggests that Oken was motivated by the Christian precept to love his neighbour, and to Oken

---

\* Canon Rudd was Vicar of St. Mary's from 1970 to 1984.

15

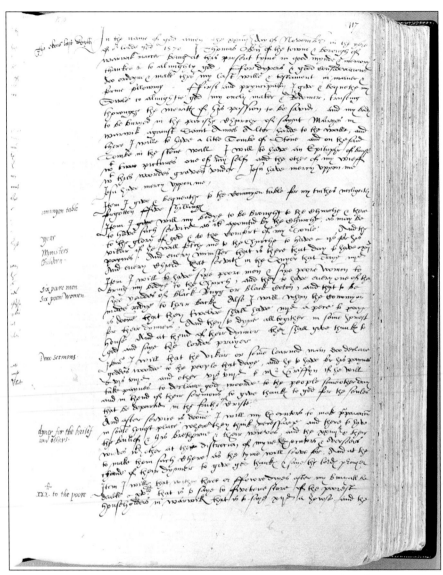

*Thomas Oken's Will as it appears in the 'Black Book'*
*(Warwick Town Council and Record Office CR3695)*

neighbours included not only friends, acquaintances and the deserving poor, but the undeserving poor as well. "There might be a clue in the bequest he made to Harris' wife: 'I will and bequeath to Thomas Harris' wife and every one of her children that she had by Thomas Harris, 12 pence apiece'. It looks as though Thomas Harris – and presumably his companion, Nicholas Morrell – was a ne'er-do-well who neglected his wife and children, and had very little to recommend him. Thomas Oken felt that he couldn't leave them out altogether, but wanted to make it perfectly clear that he wasn't leaving them money because he approved of their way of life, but *for God's sake only*".

And so the will disposes of all his money and personal possessions. All this appears to be in cash and valuables. No mention is made of any goods: presumably he had given up his business interests on retirement. No mention either is made of his considerable house property because that was dealt with in two deeds which Oken had executed a few weeks after the will in January 1571. These were very formal legal documents in contrast to the will which, as we have seen, was a very human document, obviously written by the man himself.

# — 5 —

# *Two Deeds*

Today there is one set of Trustees for Oken's Charity, but for centuries there were two because of the apparently complicated, but effective, legal way in which Oken set about things. By a deed of 'feoffment' dated January 1st 1571 he granted all his property to Thomas Burges, the Bailiff, and five other 'feoffees', William Huddisson, John Butler, John Fisher, Richard Broke and Thomas Powell, and the duty of managing these estates rested with them. However, by an indenture of January 20th that year Richard Roo and·eleven others were to be responsible each year for performing certain covenants: they were to distribute after his death the monies obtained from the rents of those properties for the benefit of the town in the ways which Oken specified. Interestingly, this second body of trustees included both executors of Oken's will, Robert Phillips and Thomas Cawdrey, and three of the overseers, William Frekenton, Robert Sheldon and John Green. We have also seen that Fisher and Powell were overseers.

According to the first deed Oken's property consisted of "all those his messuages (*i.e. houses and gardens*), lands, tenements, cottages, houses, edifices, stables, dovehouses, gardens, orchards, meadows and hereditaments (*inherited property*) with the appurtenances (*appendages*), situate in the towns, suburbs, fields and hamlets of Warwick, Baddesley, Beausale, and Harbury in the county of Warwick, and all other his lands and tenements in the realm of England." This property included three houses to be adapted as almshouses in the long since disappeared Pebble Lane (which ran from New Street to our Northgate Street); five houses in the Square (roughly equivalent to Old Square today); a house in Church Street; two houses in Sheep Street, now Northgate Street; two houses in Bridewell Lane (our Barrack Street) which were later sold for extensions to the prison and the monies invested; four houses in the Saltisford (at the foot of the northern side of North Rock);* a barn and a stable in Hogsford (West Rock); five houses and a public house in Cow Lane (our

---

\* Thomas Facer, the Yorkshire stonemason who introduced Methodism into Warwick two hundred years ago in 1801, could have been a lodger or a near neighbour of later tenants here.

Brook Street); eight houses, another inn and a stable in Friars Street; five acres of Lammas (Common) Land near West Street; a kitchen and a laundry in High Street (later to be rented by the Earl of Warwick!); Oken's residence and two other houses in Castle Street; two houses in Mill Street; six houses and over thirty acres of fields at Bridge End; a house in Southam Street, later part of Bridge End (which left the end of the old bridge to connect with our Myton Road); four houses in St. Nicholas Church Street; a house in Smith Street; and three houses and a close in Coten End. Out in the country Oken also owned a coppice and a 55 acre farm with farmhouse at Beausale; a meadow at Baddesley Clinton; and a tenement and three acre close at Harbury.

All tenants had to pay rent in cash, but interestingly most of them also had to pay something extra in the form of livestock. For example, the licensee of the Cross Keys public house in Friars Street was required to provide two pullets or 3s. 6d. in lieu. If you only rented a garden a ham was sufficient, but the farmer at Beausale had to provide two pigs and two geese – and it was specified they be fat – or 17s. in lieu. Some of this would have been provided for Oken's Feast which we shall consider in detail later on.

Instituting this annual Feast in his memory for the Bailiff, the twelve principal burgesses and 24 wardsmen, Oken directed that £1 should be provided out of the Charity towards it, and the Vicar of St. Mary's should be paid 6s. 8d. for the Sermon preceding it (there is some duplication in will and deed), and that 3s. 4d. be distributed among the poor of Warwick that day. The poor were also to have £4 distributed among them each Christmas and Easter. And six poor people (either married couples or two men or two women sharing) who were to live rent free in the three Pebble Lane almshouses were also to receive £1. 4s. between them each year "upon condition that the said six poor almspeople should daily pray for the preservation of the Queen." Two of them each year were to have "garments of rug or black cloth". "Upon the said garments there should be set as well at the backs, as before on the breast, two letters of white cloth, that is to say a T and an O for Thomas Oken."

Besides providing for the less well off, Oken had in mind that the income from his properties could also be used for educational purposes, for the benefit of the Church, for keeping the infrastructure of the town in good repair, and also for a little recreation.

Oken directed that £2 a year was to be used to augment the salary of the Grammar School master and a further £2 to augment the pay of the schoolmaster who taught the poor men's children and 'petties', young boys trained at the old Choir School. These two schools had previously been run by the Dean and Chapter of St. Mary's, but when St. Mary's ceased to be a collegiate foundation in 1544, both had been displaced, the Grammar School from St. John's Church in the Market Place and the Choir School from the College adjacent to St. Mary's in the Butts. Since

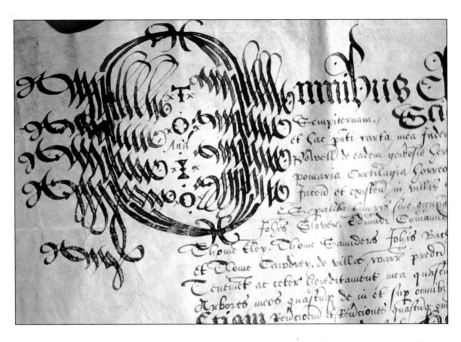

*Decorated capital and Oken's signature on Deed of Feoffment, Jan.1st, 1571*
*(Record Office CR2758/3)*

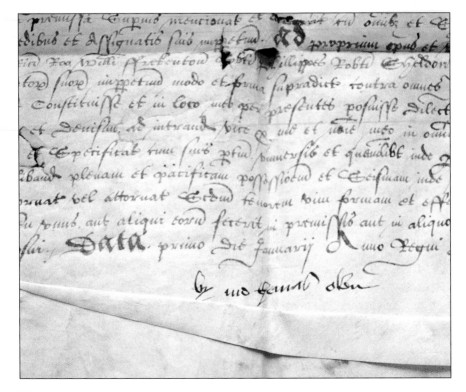

that time both schools had met in Oken's beloved Guildhall, so he must have had a special affection for them. Indeed, since the Grammar School was to evolve into the Warwick School of today, he can be said to have helped to save 'Warwick' School from extinction, as his Trustees were to do as well three centuries later. A few years after Leicester acquired the buildings for his Hospital (we are not told how the boys and the old soldiers got on in the meantime), the Grammar School transferred about 1577, as George Tibbits has conclusively shown, to St. Peter's Chapel over the East Gate, one of the properties given to the Corporation by the Earl in recompense.* The 'petties' Choir School may have moved to a room over the porch of the old Church at this time, but it was also later to transfer to the East Gate after the Grammar School had left there.

The Vicar of St. Mary's was to receive £2 for preaching four sermons on particular occasions – on the first Sunday in Lent and the Sundays immediately before St. John the Baptist's Day, Michaelmas and Christmas – and 12s. was to be shared each year among three choristers for singing in St. Mary's.

Ten shillings was set aside annually for paving the market place, and the beadle was to receive 3s. 4d. for cleaning the town centre and keeping beggars and vagabonds off the streets at the same time. A further 2s. was set aside to keep the public wells at the West Gate and in the Saltisford in

---

\* A. F. Leach in his "History of Warwick School" believed the Grammar School moved back to its old premises of St. John's Church, but, if so, this did not occur until later.

*Opening part of Oken's Indenture, Jan.20th, 1571 (Record Office CR2758/5)*

good repair, 1s. towards the maintenance of a third well which Oken wanted built in the Castle Street area, and 10s. towards the upkeep of the Emscote bridge. Finally as far as the roads were concerned there was 10s. for repairing Wedgnock Lane. This, not the Coventry Road, was then the main road out of town to the north, the route by which Queen Elizabeth departed for Kenilworth Castle.

On a merrier note, five shillings was to be devoted to bonfires and 1s. 8d. for the young men who cut down the Whitsuntide ivy at the High Cross where the four roads met.

There was 3s. 4d.. for a herdsman of St. Mary's who looked after people's cattle on the Common, and finally there was an honorarium of 4s. for those who collected the rents and distributed the various grants "to make merry withal at some banquet."

Anything left over from the income from the rents after all these commitments had been met was to be stored in a chest in St. Mary's and could be distributed among the poor and needy in time of war or high taxation. If there was no such need, such monies could contribute to the repair and upkeep of Warwick's lifeline of the "great bridge" over the river which we with hindsight realise should have been a top priority in the minds of the burgesses.

# — 6 —

# *Memorials, Chests and Silver*

As we have seen, Thomas Oken stipulated in his will that he should be buried in St. Mary's "against St. Anne's altar hard by the wall" and that a brass of himself and his wife be placed on the tomb. This was accordingly done, with the inscription underneath the brass reading:

Of your charyte give thanks for the Soules of Thomas Oken & Jone
  his Wyff on whose soules Jesus hath mcy   Jesus hath mcy amen
Remember ye charyte for the pore for ever   A dm MCCCCCLXXIII

(A piece of the brass has been replaced. It is believed that "give thanks for the souls", a phrase more acceptable to Protestants, was substituted for the Catholic rendering of "pray for the souls." In any case it was now illegal to pray for the dead)

Unfortunately St. Anne's Chapel was destroyed in the Great Fire of 1694, but the brass was saved, and when the church was restored it was put up on the wall of the south transept in the new nave. Beneath it the restorers added a second inscription in gold lettering on stone:

To ye Memory of MR THOMAS OKEN an Ornament to his own & a blessing to Ages succeeding / This Monument defaced by ye late dreadfull Fire is reerected & dedicated by his FEOFFEES / The MAYOR & ALDERMEN of this BOROUGH

Whose Industry being Born Here of mean Parents was so bless'd in ye Trade he / exercised of a Mercer that 37MO H8 (*i.e. 1545 – 46*) he was Master of the Gild of ye holy Trinity & St. George / now ye Hospital of Rt E of Leicester 5to P & Marrae (*i.e. 1557 – 58*) Bailiff of this BOROUGH & dying 15to Eliz (*i.e. 1573*) / gave to pious and Charitable Uses Here an Estate then lett for less yn 20£ p(*er*) An(*num*) now by / ye just care of his Feoffees advancd notwithstanding The loss

23

*The Memorial to Thomas and Joan Oken in St. Mary's*

of several Houses by / ye late Fire to more than 100£ p(*er*) An(*num*) also 100£ to purchase Land to enlarge ye Common / 30£ to ye Poor 10£ to 30 poor Maidens for Marriages 94 Ounces of wrought Plate / for ye Use of ye Bailiffs successively & to ye Boroughs of STRATFORD & / BANBURY 40£ each to be lent to honest Tradesmen. Vide Dugdale War.

This CHARITY Reader was so wisely instituted & ye TRUST so honestly executed yt if to / Thy FAITH thou art disposd to join GOOD WORKS thou needst seek no farther for / Model or encouragement – or Opportunity for YE HAVE YE POOR WITH YOU ALWAYS

The inscriptions were, however, rather high up on the wall where they could scarcely be read. But in 1972, at the suggestion of Canon Julian Rudd, the Church Council and Oken's Trustees agreed to move the memorials to their present position at the entrance to the north transept, just outside the Regimental Chapel which now occupies the site of St. Anne's Chapel. And so brass and stone to Thomas Oken were appropriately moved as near as possible to his last resting place in time for the four hundredth anniversary of his death.

We have seen that Oken stipulated in his will that "the poor man's chest stand fast by where I shall be buried" – secured with eight locks, the keys of which were to be held by the bailiff, three other burgesses and four wardsmen. "And I will that my executors shall appoint some other chest

*The Chest reputedly belonging to Thomas Oken*

*A selection of Oken's silver*

*Oken's Mace still carried by the Assistant Serjeant-at-Arms*

to stand in the place." Herein lies a mystery. As early as 1792 there was no chest in St. Mary's belonging to the Charity, but there are now three chests in existence. It is said that the one by the vestry door belongs to the Parish, the one in the south aisle is that of Oken, and the one in the Court House, although marked T.O., is Eyffler's. Another theory is that this last chest, which is believed to have been in St. Mary's at one time, could have been the one made in accordance with Oken's instructions. It has twelve locks, not eight, but this may be because there were eight wards requiring keys, not four as mentioned in the will.

The original silver mentioned in Oken's will was sold in 1752, but 'Oken's Mace', strictly a Recorder's Mace, is carried on ceremonial occasions on behalf of the Recorder's successor the Town Clerk. It may have been manufactured in the middle of the sixteenth century, although George Tibbits says it could possibly have been made about 1683 and may have replaced an earlier one. Further items have been purchased or donated over the years – and some replaced after theft a few years ago – and today, in addition to the Mace, Oken's silver consists of Oken's chest in miniature, a silver platter, a wine jug, two large beer mugs, one with a lid and one without, three small beer mugs, one large and two small sugar casters, a small silver urn, twelve large spoons and three small spoon rests. These 28 items are held by the Town Clerk at the Court House.

# — 7 —

# *Nicholas Eyffler and his Charity*

The Charity of Thomas Oken's friend Nicholas Eyffler is now one with Oken's, and its inception must therefore be mentioned at this stage.

Nicholas Eyffler was a German immigrant from Osnabruck in Westphalia. He was born about 1512, and settled in London probably for economic reasons rather then religious persecution. He is believed to have come to Warwick under the patronage of Sir Thomas Lucy who was building Charlecote and to have supplied glass both for Lucy and for the Earl of Leicester at Kenilworth Castle. Certainly he carried on a very successful business as a glazier at a time when glass for windows was becoming increasingly common. He became a 'denizen' of this country (not quite a naturalised Englishman) in March 1562, and lived first in or near the Market Place and later in two houses in Jury Street.

By his will dated January 14th 1591, Eyffler gave his property to two Trustees, Robert West and Thomas Camell. After the death of his wife (like Oken he was childless), they were to rent out his second house on the south side of Jury Street for £1 a year, initially to his brother-in-law's family called Goldsmith, who were also to rent his Meakin's Close property in West Street for ten shillings a year. These rents were to be paid to the collectors of Oken's Charity and the money was to be applied in the same way as Oken's for the relief of the poor.

By his will Eyffler also instructed that on a third property belonging to him, a close on the Back Hills (our Castle Hill), two timber-framed barns should be converted and extended into four almshouses for old women, unmarried women to be given preference over widows. In the event the four houses were built of brick on the site (early examples for Warwick) at a cost of £72. 5s .2d., and when they were completed in November 1597 the first occupants were four widows and four spinsters who, living two to a house as in Oken's almshouses, were also given a dress ("a new frize gowne" – a kind of coarse woollen cloth) and one shilling each. For their maintenance, the charity's income totalled £3. 6s. 8d. a year, made up of

16s. 8d. in rent from one barn, £1 from the other, the £1 from the Jury Street house and the 10s. from Meakins Close.

When the Great Fire of Warwick destroyed the three Oken almshouses in Pebble Lane, that Charity built six additional ones for twelve inmates in 1696 on to the southern end of these Eyffler cottages on what continued to be Eyffler land. The inscription upon them reads:

> Whereas 3 Alms Houses standing in Pebble Lane in Warwick
> which Received 6 Poor Persons
> given by MR THOMAS OKEN Deceased
> were burnt by the Dreadful Fire upon the 5th Day of Sept. 1694
> these Alms Houses to Receive 12 Persons
> were by the Charity of the said THOMAS OKEN
> Built upon the Ground given by MR NICH. IFFELER Deceased
> to the same Charitable Office
> by the Feoffees of the said Charity
> upon the 20th Day of May Anno. Dom. 1696

Incidentally, these almshouses did not appear 'so high and lifted up' in those days: the hill was lowered in the 1790s to allow the road to approach the new bridge over the river less steeply.

West and Camell had passed their responsibilities over to an extended body of eight Trustees in 1593, and that Trust was renewed from time to time, but before the end of the seventeenth century we find the Oken

*The Oken and Eyffler Almshouses in Castle Hill in olden times*

Trustees acting on behalf of the Eyffler Charity. (Hence the building of Oken almshouses on Eyffler land.) However, at the time of the Municipal Corporations Act of 1835 the poorer Eyffler's Charity was separated from Oken's and managed by the Municipal Trustees. This unsatisfactory state of affairs as far as the almshouses were concerned continued until the Charity Commissioners' Scheme of August 24th 1956 transferred the management of Eyffler's Charity to the Oken Trustees, and all ten Castle Hill almshouses (Nos. 1 – 4 Eyffler's, Nos. 5 – 10 Oken's) were then thoroughly modernised. Finally, as we shall see later, the two charities were completely amalgamated in 1988.

*Portrait of Thomas Oken's friend, Nicholas Eyffler*
*(no portrait of Oken himself exists)*

# — 8 —

# *Oken's Feast*

Provision was made for the Feast in both will and deed. According to the will, "After service is done I will my executors to make preparation in some honest place where they think necessary, and there to have the Bailiff and his brethren and their wives and the twenty-four and their wives with other at the discretion of mine executors and overseers, to make them such cheer as the time will serve for, and at the end of their dinner to give God thanks and say the Lord's Prayer."

According to the deed, "Also yearly, after the said service and sermon, at some decent and honest place within the said town, cause a dinner to be prepared as well for the Bailiff and twelve principal burgesses of the said town, as for three of the most honest and substantial commoners of any of the eight wards within the said town, to make merry withal, and distribute out of the revenues of the said lands, yearly, towards the charge thereof 20s., and in the end of the said dinner to say the Lord's Prayer, and to praise God for the soul of the said Thomas Oken, Joan his wife, and all Christian souls departed out of this transitory world."

The first Feast – in 1574 – took place before the dispute between executors and overseers had been settled, and was far from the pleasant occasion it should have been. In the course of his speech in praise of Thomas Oken, John Fisher remarked that he wished the executors had carried out their duties as well as the collectors of the rents had done. Robert Phillips who was present immediately challenged this allegation. "Nay," said Fisher, "you have not done so, but have done most falsely and far otherwise than you ought to have done." "Wherein?" asked Phillips. "In all things," said Fisher, "and mainly in that you have neither paid the legacies nor proved his will, but have most shamelessly sworn that you have proved the will, whereas you have proved a false will, like wretches and men of no credit." "Nay," said Phillips, "we are of as good credit as you, and do as truly as you, and have I this for lending thee my money." "Lending me thy money," said Fisher, "thou hast lent me none but that I pay truly for to thee like a vile usuring knave." "Knave?" queried Phillips. "Yea," answered Fisher, "thou are a false, forsworn and perjured knave, and that I will prove and stand to it. And I trust to see thine ears nailed of the pillory like a false crippling knave." Phillips angrily started to get up,

*The Great Hall of the Lord Leycester Hospital where the Feast takes place today*

*Poster and Tickets for Oken's Feast in 1861 (Record Office
CR1618/WA6/229/3 )*

but was restrained, which made him even more heated. "Have you brought me hither to murder me?" he asked, threatening Fisher.

Phillips did in fact later bring an action for slander against Fisher, claiming £100 damages, and Fisher brought a counter-claim for perjury, for which Phillips appears to have had to pay. So Oken's Feast did not get off to a very good start!

No details survive concerning other early Feasts, though the assumption is that they were held regularly because Thomas Oken was so respected by his contemporaries. It would also be as natural for them as it was for Oken to regard the Feast as a continuation of the old Guild Feasts. It was also an Audit Dinner.

Thomas Kemp, however, has extracted from the Black Book an interesting account of the Feast of 1657 which was a tripartite gathering attended by the civic heads of Stratford and Banbury as well as those of Warwick. Conditions had been attached to the £40 Oken gave to these two towns in his will: they were to invest the money and apply the interest chiefly for the benefit of their poor (except for an amount to be spent on a dinner on feast days there too, with 3s. 4d. for the preacher of a sermon – half Warwick's rate), and then every three or four years they had to satisfy the Bailiff of Warwick that the money had been properly applied and was still in their hands! And so we learn that on June 6th 1657 the Bailiffs of Banbury and Stratford met the Bailiff of Warwick (the title Mayor dates from 1664) at the Great Swan (now the Warwick Arms), and, "after some friendly salutations and a glass of wine or two", they went up the street to St. Mary's where a Banbury cleric, Rev. Bernard Maunder, Vicar of Cropredy, preached the sermon for his 3s. 4d.. Afterwards they returned to the hostelry for dinner where Rev. Richard Venner, the Vicar of St. Mary's, said grace and concluded with the Lord's Prayer as required by Oken's will. Afterwards the Bailiffs of Banbury and Stratford formally presented their £40 each to the Bailiff of Warwick, and the monies were returned to them equally formally – uncounted.

It seems likely that this excellent practice of a joint Feast was held periodically at least until 1714, but that it ceased during the period 1734 – 1769 when Warwick Corporation was under a cloud cast by proceedings in Chancery when all their property was sequestered. However, the Feast itself continued to be held annually, and until the end of the eighteenth century Oken's £1 limit on expenditure was faithfully observed, presumably because of the rent received in produce from the Charity's tenants. By 1826, however, £33. 2s. 5d. was spent on the Feast, and in spite of the censure of His Majesty's Commissioners that year, it was still £27. 10s. 4d. in 1828.

In the nineteenth century the Feast was held at the various hostelries in turn. For example, in September 1873 it was held at the Old Bowling Green Hotel, and the bill for 37 dinners came to £14. 16s.. One year in which the sequence was broken was 1887. At their September meeting the Feoffees "resolved for the present in consequence of the recent catastrophe caused by the Bank failure to postpone the holding of the Feast". Greenways Bank had collapsed, and George Cattell Greenway was the Charity's Receiver.

The Feast, now held in the autumn, continued up to 1913 (with the exception of the years 1899, 1905, 1906, 1907 and 1911 – as we shall see the Charity's finances were then in a parlous condition), but apart from 1919 it was not held again after the First World War until 1924 when the not excessive figure of £30 for that time was voted towards expenses. The Feast then continued up to 1933, though on three occasions the Wardsmen held it when the Feoffees did not want to, and on three other occasions the diners paid the costs themselves. However, the Charity Commissioners' Scheme of 1934 pegged the figure back to Oken's original £1, so that the Feast was not resumed until 1952 with the diners meeting their own expenses. George Tibbits was responsible for this revival, and each year until his death in 1968 he proposed the toast of "the pious memory of Thomas Oken and Joan his wife", finding something new to say about him each time. He was also responsible for making it a joint Feast for a number of years. The Mayors of Stratford and Banbury were again invited, together with the Lord Mayor of Coventry and the Master of the Fellowship of Cappers of Coventry, because of their towns' connections with Thomas Oken. And in 1973 there were two dinners: the usual Feast at the Lord Leycester Hospital in the January and a Special Festival at the Guy Nelson Hall on July 30th to commemorate the 400th anniversary of Oken's death. The Trustees also arranged a second banquet, again in the Guy Nelson Hall, on July 29th 1995 to celebrate the 450th anniversary of the Charter which Oken secured for the town.

Whilst it is sad to record that down the years certain Trustees had allowed far more than the £1 Oken allowed to be spent on the Feast, it is refreshing to find that a far different approach was now being taken.

The Scheme of 1988 amalgamating Oken's and Eyffler's Charities provided for an increase in the annual payments in connection with the Feast. The Rector was to receive £20 for his sermon rather then the 6s. 8d. decreed by Oken, and the choir, choirmaster and organist £120, with a further £20 for incidentals in connection with the service. Additional sums include £20 for the Beadle in connection with the procession, £10 each to the preachers of the four sermons on specific Sundays during the year, and £100 to the Mayor for distribution among the poor. Moreover, all these sums could be increased on application to the Charity Commissioners: each specific figure is followed by the phrase "or such other sum as the Commissioners may from time to time approve".

The one 'anomaly' was that the expenditure on the Feast itself was limited without qualification to Oken's original £1. George Tibbits had argued some years earlier that as Oken himself obviously wished the Feast to continue and that as £1 represented about one-twentyfifth of the Charity's income in Oken's day it should be substantially increased, and indeed the Commissioners were willing to allocate more. But, resolutely refusing to profit in any way from the Charity themselves, the Trustees unanimously decided against any increase. That £1 is probably equivalent to about £1,000 today!

The Feast, the successor of the old Guild Feast and Oken's bequest of good fellowship, returned to its original home in 1955 and continues to be held regularly on the last Friday in January each year in the Great Hall of the Lord Leycester Hospital, a fitting venue, for it was the meeting place both of the Guild and of the Corporation of Oken's day.

Moreover, the Feast is as well organised as it is enjoyable. In 1982 "it was felt that some of the speeches had been unnecessarily long, but nonetheless enjoyable. The Clerk indicated that it was his proposal in future years to have a timetable for speeches limiting their length to a reasonable term." The fact that the event is often oversubscribed demonstrates the effectiveness of such good ordering.

*Oken's House*

*The Plaque on Oken's House*

# — 9 —

# *Oken's House*

After Agnes Catur's death the House in Castle Street where Oken lived and died would have been let out to tenants by the Trustees. In 1826, for example, Joseph Penn paid an annual rent of £21. 8s. and two capons or 3s. 6d. in lieu.

In 1864, "with characteristic Victorian bad taste and thoroughness" (to quote George Tibbits), the walls of Oken's House were covered with plaster and false timbers. At the same time two small gables were added on the eastern side, fronting Castle Street, and the following inscription was placed on a commemorative tablet:

THOMAS OKEN
A mercer of this Borough
who died A.D. 1573
gave this house (in which he resided)
together with other property situate in Warwick
Baddesley Clinton Beawsale and Harbury for certain charitable uses
The Estate is managed by a body of Feoffees
who after making certain specific payments
and providing for necessary repairs
hand over the surplus according to the intention of the donor
to 24 Wardsmen and 13 Nominees of the Town Council
who make weekly payments to certain poor persons
from time to time selected
as proper recipiemts of the Charity
The house has been restored
as nearly as practicable
to its original state and appearance
A.D. 1864

The house was properly restored again in 1949 – 50 at a cost of £1048. 16s. 5d. when the false timbering was removed, the plaster stripped off and the two false gables removed. At the same time the stone mentioned above was turned with its lettering to the wall and the present inscription added:

Here lived
THOMAS OKEN
a great benefactor to Warwick
He died here on
the 29th July 1573

In the 1860s and 1870s there was a private school in Castle Street run in turn by three maiden ladies, Miss Cooke, Miss Summerville and Miss Crump, who taught needlework and the three Rs. It has been said that the school met in Oken's House, though none of the ladies is listed as a tenant of the Charity. Indeed in the late nineteenth century the House was a baker's shop for many years. Its use was changed to an antique dealer's in the early years of the twentieth century. In 1955 Joy Robinson acquired the lease for her extensive collection of dolls and toys, and it has been a Dolls' Museum ever since. On Joy's death in 1978 it was maintained by her sister Peggy Nesbitt and her husband for a number of years, but in 1987 the collection was bought by the County Council for £55,600 thanks to a generous donation of £16,000 from the King Henry VIII Charity and other donations from public bodies, local businesses and the general public. The building is now leased to the County Council and the Dolls' Museum is part of its Museum Service.

# — 10 —

# *Oken's Charity in 1694*

It is convenient to look at Oken's Charity at certain specific dates, and one such is 1694. The Great Fire of London in 1665 was no unique event. In those days of timber framed buildings with thatched roofs many a town had a serious conflagration, and the Great Fire of Warwick occurred on September 5th 1694 when the whole of High Street, Church Street, Northgate Street and other parts of the town were totally destroyed. Even the nave and tower of St. Mary's went up in flames because the distraught citizens brought their smouldering belongings with them when they sought refuge there. In such circumstances even Oken's leather buckets were of no avail.

It is difficult to identify all the individual houses, but we can be reasonably sure that only about a quarter of the Charity's properties were burnt down because many of them were fortunately off-centre. The three almshouses in Pebble Lane, valued at £60, were destroyed and Elizabeth Dyer, Sarah Cooper, Anne Dunne, Mary Bolton, and William and Mary Pestle rendered homeless as a result. So were Phyllis Woodward and Ann Matthews in other Oken properties in the Lane which itself disappeared in the subsequent town centre planning. The houses of Thomas Newsham on the west side of Church Street and Sarah Edwards on the other side went up in flames as did that of John Byker in Sheep Street (Northgate Street), whilst another tenant, shoemaker John Atterbury, also in Sheep Street, lost goods to the value of £209. 3s. 4d. Not all these properties were rebuilt: indeed, in September 1696 the Trustees were paid £19. 4s. 4$\frac{1}{2}$d. for the compulsory purchase of a piece of their land to form the new Old Square.

Away from the epicentre other tenants also lost house and home. Matthew Busby's Sign of the Peacock in Joyce Pool or Bridewell Lane was burnt down as was a kitchen rented by Dorothy Weale and her son Fulke on the south side of High Pavement (High Street). Though the direction of the wind mercifully prevented the fire from reaching Oken's own House, it did just catch the corner of Castle Street and gut part of the house of another shoemaker, Thomas Marriott.

Joseph Blissett, George Webb, Richard Hands, Aaron Rogers, William Tarver and Charles Hickes, the Trustees of the day, obviously had their work cut out. Indeed, despite nation-wide contributions to the town, they did not have sufficient ready money for such an eventuality and had to borrow themselves, because there is a record of their repaying £300 to the treasurer of the disaster fund in April 1699.

As already related, two years after the Fire the Charity replaced the three almshouses destroyed in Pebble Lane with six adjacent to the Eyffler cottages on the Back Hills.

The 'petties' Choir School lost its home in St. Mary's in the Fire and transferred to the East Gate. In 1699 the Grammar School moved into the old college buildings in the Butts adjacent to St. Mary's. It either made way for the Choir School at East Gate or had itself been made homeless when the Fire destroyed St. John's Church in the Market Place.

# — 11 —

# *Oken's Charity in 1826*

Much of interest on Oken's Charity can be gleaned from the "Report of His Majesty's Commissioners for Inquiring into the Public Charities of the Borough of Warwick" of August 1826.

The properties held by the Trustees were substantially the same as Oken had left them. Apart from the almshouses built on the Back Hills to replace those destroyed in Pebble Lane by the Great Fire, there were only five alterations in two hundred and fifty years, and those did not occur until the latter half of the eighteenth century.

In 1765 the Trustees acquired from the Earl of Warwick a house in Church Street producing a rent of £9 per annum in place of one of its six houses at Bridge End with a yearly value of only £6: no doubt the earl was wanting that particular property near the castle, so the Trustees got a bargain. Then in June 1773 they obtained land at Myton which included Stud Farm and the area occupied by the houses built in Myton Crescent whose freeholds the Trustees did not sell to the householders until 1961.

In February 1792 the Charity gave the Earl a house and garden off Southam Street (that part of our Bridge End which ran east from the old bridge) in exchange for two houses in Warytree Street or Gallows Street – that part of Bridge End which ran south-east from the old bridge and led to Gallows Hill (the Whitnash road) where executions took place in olden times. "Two messuages, with a malthouse, garden and appurtenances belonging to them" in Bridewell Lane (our Barrack Street) were sold in the same month to the Warwickshire Justices for £333. 6s. 8d. (plus £1 a year rent on fourteen years of an unexpired 99 years lease) for the purpose of enlarging the County Gaol. This property, believed to have been a public house called "The Peacock" (a connection with the Castle?), would have been adjacent to the Abbotsford and have extended back to the site of the present County Council Chamber. Out of this money the Trustees spent £105 buying a house in Pillory Street (part of our Old Square).

Finally, in December 1798 the Trustees exchanged a house in Smith Street for one in Queenwell Street (Friars Street).

These were the only property transactions of the Charity – half a dozen, all exchanges – in some two hundred and fifty years. Some property in Cross Street may also have been acquired between 1826 and 1879. But compare this with the wholesale and (with hindsight) disastrous sell off of over fifty of their houses in 1879, a subject which we shall deal with in a later chapter.

The accounts of the day show three types of payments: ordinary payments relating for the most part to items actually stipulated by Oken himself; extraordinary payments to contractors for services rendered – carpenters, masons, painters, glaziers and the like; and finally payments to the poor of Warwick. In the eighteenth century these latter had been one off payments of 2s., 2s. 6d. or 3s. to three hundred or so individuals. But in 1772 – 73 Ann Goode receives 10s. 6d in monthly payments, and two years later 21 other poor folk receive weekly payments for the whole or part of the year. Thereafter the one off payments tail off, and by the turn of the century 31 people are receiving 2s. a week. The number of recipients increases to about 80 at one stage, and in 1832 some of them begin to receive 4s.a week.

Extra payments at this time include:

| | |
|---|---|
| "To the Cook for dressing the Dinner | 5s. |
| To the Beadle for summoning the Wardsmen | 1s. |
| To the Porter for keeping the Poor out at the Feast | 1s. |
| To Ale at and after Dinner | £1" |

The porter was paid for his task as late as 1840.

Finally, the herdsman must have earned his 3s. 4d. well into the nineteenth century, because there are entries in the list of tenants noting 'Cow', 'Horse', 'Horse and Cow' and 'One Beast'. The office of herdsman was not abolished until the Warwick Corporation Act of 1948 extinguished common rights when the Borough Council took over St. Mary's Lands. Older Warwick residents can still remember when horses were set free to graze on the Common.

# — 12 —

# *Municipal Reform*

T he Municipal Corporations Act of 1835, that flagship policy of a reforming administration, proved to be a mixed blessing for Warwick, exacerbating as it did the already strained relations between the two sets of trustees. The administration of the Charity was in the hands of a number of Feoffees on the one hand (a minimum of 16 when the Trust was renewed), and 24 Commoners (three from each of eight wards and therefore also called Wardsmen) and the Mayor and twelve principal burgesses on the other. However, one of the provisions of the new Act was that the care of the property of local charities (though strangely not Eyffler's) should be separated from the administration of local government. A complicated struggle for power followed. In January 1837 the Whig Borough Council appointed 13 Whig nominees to add to the 17 Tory and seven Whig Wardsmen to give them a small majority in the second body. However, it so happened that the Trust had last been renewed in 1820 and the number of Feoffees had fallen to the five needed for renewal. This gave the Tory Receiver the chance to renew the Trust that March with four old Feoffees (one retired) and 35 new ones, all Tory! This meant not only were the two bodies to be at daggers drawn until the political composition of the Council changed in Novermber 1840, but there were now no less than 76 people responsible for Oken's Charity – doubtless one of the reasons for the popularity of the Feast in the nineteenth century!

Although they appointed the Wardsmen, the Feoffees rarely held joint meetings with the Wardsmen and Nominees, and both bodies kept separate account and minute books. Three main concerns appear in the minutes of the Wardsmen and Nominees at this time. One was the selection of deserving boys from poor families to attend the Bablake or 'Boblic' School, the successor to the school for 'petties' of Oken's day which continued to meet over the East Gate. The Grammar School master still received the standard £2, now much reduced in value, from the Charity, but the Bablake master received an additional salary of £8. 13s. 4d., plus more for books, Bibles and stationery. And, for example, in July 1850, "It is ordered that Mr. Palmer of the Market Square, Draper, do supply the cloth necessary for the coats and caps for the Boblic Boys on

Oken's foundation and that the same be made by James Spooner who hath hitherto made the same." £1. 10s. was also set aside to provide the boys with their own special annual dinner.

That same minute of July 1850 mentioned above continues: "And it is ordered that Mr. Perks do supply the almswomen with gowns as usual. And it is ordered that enquiry be made for two poor women to supply vacancies at the almshouses in the Back Hills". This reveals the Wardsmen's second concern: looking after the residents of the almshouses and filling the occasional vacancies that occurred there.

Their third task was the distribution of weekly pensions to folk in need which since the end of the eighteenth century had superseded casual one-off payments. For example, in 1841 it was agreed that 29 people should receive 4s. a week, "subject to enquiry to be made of such Objects whether any of them do or have received Parochial Relief and if they have the payment to such Object or Objects to be discontinued". As late as 1890 – 91 the pay sheet of the distributors of the money was headed 'Oken's Objects' (later it became 'Oken's Recipients'). Language may have changed over the years, and they were after all objects of charity, but how the description sticks in our throats – as does the entry 'Widow Smith' without the men's benefit of Christian names! And would we appreciate being described as 'Decayed tradesman'? Incidentally, the recipients were expected to accompany the Trustees to the service in St. Mary's before the Feast to show their gratitude, though not to join them for dinner!

However, there is one pleasing bit of business to record mid-century. By a Deed of Exchange in November 1848 the Feoffees conveyed to the Earl of Warwick seven houses in Bridge End and three in Mill Street in exchange for four houses in Smith Street and eight in Cross Street. Obviously the Earl was happy to be 'consolidating' his properties, and it might seem to us that the Charity was losing 'des. res.'. However, the rental of the property surrendered was £64. 18s., while that of the property received in exchange totalled £118, so the Feoffees seem to have made a good bargain!

And, although separate minute books continued to be kept, by the 1870s Feoffees and Wardsmen were holding joint meetings, and a more amicable state of affairs existed. Which was just as well, for the Charity was about to fall on hard times.

# — 13 —

# The Decline of the Charity

Two decisons of the Trustees in the late nineteenth century were to have a deleterious effect upon the Charity. Both turned out in retrospect to have been financially unwise, and the one to support middle class education seems to have been contrary to the spirit of Oken's intentions.

The problem concerned an ailing Warwick School which fell on hard times in the nineteenth century. In 1832 there were only fifteen boys in the school, and on an earlier occasion only ten! They were taught classics on the premises in the Butts, but had to go to Bablake School to be taught the three Rs by the master there! And no love was lost between the boys of the two schools:the Warwick boys nicknamed the Bablake boys "bobdogs".

In December 1869 a joint meeting of the trustees of a number of Warwick charities had appealed to all local charities to support education. A worthy cause, but in this case it was education for the middle classes rather than for the poor – education for the poor was to be furthered by the Education Act the following year. The Oken Trustees unanimously resolved to increase their giving to education to £100, and this extra expenditure was only slighly offset by the discontinuance of payments for the upkeep of the Market Place, Wedgnock Lane, the Saltisford Well and the paving under the Gates for which the Borough Council now took over responsibility. And in February 1872, in place of the limited payments formerly made to Bablake and Warwick Schools, the Trustees agreed to give £200 per annum – in effect an increase of £198 to Warwick School – to a new body called the King's Schools Foundation which was eventually set up in August 1876 (Warwick School would move in 1879 to its brand new premises in the Myton Road), and in return they were granted what George Tibbits calls "the somewhat doubtful privilege" of appointing one of the School Governors, a right it still enjoys today.

The last boy was selected by the Wardsmen for Bablake in February 1875; the school closed in the summer; the boys were transferred elsewhere; and the Charity's education of the poor ceased. In 1875 according to the records the Feoffees' outgoings included £50 for the

CR 1618 / WA 16 / 13 / 1

## WARWICK, BEAUSALE, BADDESLEY CLINTON, AND HARBURY.

### Particulars, Plans, and Conditions of Sale

OF A VALUABLE

# FREEHOLD FARM

OF

## 47 Acres 0 Roods 15 Perches,

### MESSUAGES,

## TWO PUBLIC HOUSES

### AND OTHER IMPORTANT PROPERTIES,

Situate in the BOROUGH of WARWICK; and at BEAUSALE, BADDESLEY CLINTON, And HARBURY, in the COUNTY of WARWICK.

BELONGING TO THE TRUSTEES OF "THOMAS OKENS' CHARITY."

### WHICH WILL BE SOLD BY AUCTION, BY

# JOHN WILLIAM MARGETTS

### AT THE WARWICK ARMS HOTEL, WARWICK,

## ON WEDNESDAY, THE 4th DAY OF JUNE, 1879,

Commencing to the minute at Three o'clock in the Afternoon,

SUBJECT TO THE PRINTED CONDITIONS HEREUNTO ANNEXED.

To View, apply to the respective Tenants; and for further particulars, or information, to Messrs. GREENWAY and CAMPBELL, Solicitors; or the AUCTIONEER, all of Warwick.

Moody Brothers, Printers, Caxton Works, Cannon Street, Birmingham.

*Notice of the Sale of Charity Properties in 1879 (Record Office CR1618/WA6/64)* salary of the Bablake master and various other items for the school under the heading "Payments relating to the Charity School". In 1876 there were no such payments, but the first of the annual payments of £200 to the Governors of the King's Schools was included under the heading "Payments relating to Education": the words "the Charity School" were actually crossed out and the word "Education" substituted!

Oken's Trustees had been caught up in the contemporary fervour for education and like most people at the time did not see it as a service provided by the state: the £200 had indeed only been passed by the casting vote of the chairman, but the alternative was a proposal to vote £150. As a result they were strapped for cash, the cry went up that the poor were robbed, and hence a decision was made to sell property to raise ready money.

In December 1877 they decided to put most of their properties on the market. This was a disastrous decision, although to be fair to the Trustees, no one then foresaw the possibility of a fall in the value of money. Indeed they were encouraged to sell by the Charity Commissioners.* As it was, houses and land were sold in June 1879 to the value of £14,082. 18s. 6d.. Deducting costs, they were left with £13,466. 19. 3d. to invest in Consols.

The properties sold included two houses in Castle Street where the present Friendly Societies Hall now stands; two houses in Church Street and two in Northgate Street; five in Old Square, four being on the site of our old Post Office; nine cottages and the Cross Keys public house in Friars Street, all of which were demolished to make way for Westgate Close; five houses and the "White Swan" public house on the western side of Brook Street which has since been redeveloped; a coach house and stable in Theatre Street; four cottages on North Rock in the Saltisford; a coach house and stables in Joyce Pool where County Council offices are now situated; two houses and two shops in Smith Street, seven cottages in Cross Street and one in Priory Road; four cottages in St. Nicholas Church Street and five properties in Coten End; together with out of town holdings – the farm, two cottages and other fields at Beausale, the fields at Baddesley Clinton, and the cottage and fields at Harbury.

It will be noted that redevelopment has taken place in several of the areas listed. Who knows? Oken's Trustees might not have held such prime sites as the Trustees of the King Henry VIII Charity, but if they had retained all their properties until a more favourable moment they might have been some way to having been as flush with ready cash as the King Henry VIII Charity is today. That charity's sale of development land at Myton in 1986 now gives them a distributable surplus of over £1,400,000 a year!

---

* The Brabazon Campbell Report on the Charities of Warwick in 1890 reported that generally "under facilities afforded by the Commissioners, much of the landed property has been sold and converted into money, thus doing away with a great outlet for waste and jobbery".

Worse was to follow, and here I can do no better than quote directly from George Tibbits. "On the 16th June 1908 the Charity Commissioners made a Determination Order directing the transfer of £8,000 Consols to the King's Schools Foundation in satisfaction of the payment of £200 per annum. Violent objection was made by the Feoffees and Wardsmen who then realised that what had been called an annual subsidy to the School was far in excess of what it should have been when viewed in the light of Thomas Oken's Settlement which gave £2 per annum to the Grammar School Master and £2 per annum to the Choir School Master, a total of £4 out of an endowment producing just over £25 per annum, or roughly one sixth of the income of the Charity. The Feoffees, Wardsmen and Nominees of Oken's Charity had hoped after 1876 to have their promised annual subsidy for the School revised, but the Charity Commissioners refused."

"Thus there was diverted to the Schools about one half of the capital value of the Charity, for the education of children who could never by any stretch of the imagination be called 'poor men's children' in the sense that Oken used the words, and this once great endowment was reduced to no more than £6053. 0s. 8d. $2^1/_2$% Consols, some almshouses then in poor condition, Oken's House in Castle Street, some ground rents in Myton Crescent and Friars Street, and about $28^1/_2$ acres of agricultural land at Myton with a farmhouse. For many years after 1908 the Charity was virtually crippled and is only now (*1968*) beginning to recover."

No wonder the Trustees continued to insist on exercising their privilege of appointing a Governor of Warwick School. As one Trustee pointed out in September 1978, "the school itself was saved from closing at the end of the last century by funds provided out of Oken's Charity". And at a time of possible change, there appears a minute in June 1980, "In view of the fact that Oken's Charity had rescued the school itself in 1880 from financial collapse, the Clerk was requested to write to the Governors to suggest that if there was one representative from Warwick Charities then it should be Oken's". Their suggestion was accepted!

# — 14 —

# *Recovery*

The cumbersome set-up of feoffees on the one hand and wardsmen and nominees on the other, the development of Oken's creation of two sets of trustees, continued until 1934. However, by a Scheme of the Charity Commissioners of March 23rd that year these two groups were replaced by a single body of Trustees. They included such names as Arthur Tandy, head of the extensive Tandy family, Henry Norman Forbes after whom the housing estate in south-west Warwick is called, and Guy Montague Nelson of the Emscote gelatine firm from whom the Assembly Hall at Warwick School takes its name, worthy successors of the likes of Sir Michael Lakin, Thomas Kemp, Austin Edwards and Thomas Henry Kendall, the wood-carver. Presumably as many of the old feoffees and wardsmen and nominees as wished were allowed to continue as Trustees, because the original Trust consisted of the Mayor ex-officio, eleven representative Trustees to hold office until they ceased to be members of the Borough Coumcil, six co-optative Trustees entitled to hold office for life and fifteen co-optative Trustees entitled to hold office until they ceased to live or carry on business in Warwick. However, the Scheme provided for this rather unwieldy body of 33 to reduce to sixteen: the Mayor, six to be appointed by the Borough Council for a term of four years, and nine co-optative Trustees, three from each ward, to serve for eight years. Among these in mid-century were such as Alfred Knibbs, forever associated with Smith Street, Herbert Ansell of the Warwick Building Society, Philip Styles, the historian, and George Tibbits himself.

Aspects of the Charity's work changed over the years. The standard 4s. a week paid to recipients had been increased to 5s. in the 1870s, but some payments were reduced to 2s. 6d. in 1912 after the state Old Age Pensions scheme was introduced. Naturally the need for the Charity to provide such pensions declined; the 25 to 30 recipients of the earlier decades of the century fell in number; in 1949 to 1953 it was a standard 3s. 6d.; and finally in May 1953 Warwick United Charities took over the pensions of the remaining seven pensioners of Oken's who were not almspeople.

Since the Sale of 1879 the Trustees have wisely husbanded their resources. Property has only been sold where it has been in the best interests of all concerned – a couple of acres sold to the County Council

*Thomas Kemp,
transcriber of the
'Black Book'
(Juliet Homer)*

in 1958 for educational purposes (Dormer School) or land sold for housing development (houses in Myton Crescent) about the same time.

Gradual recovery allowed the refurbishment of the Castle Hill almshouses to take place in 1957–58 at a cost of £7,500. The two fireplaces side by side in each living room were removed: this peculiarity dated back to the days when each room was intended to accommodate two women! Additions were made to the original buildings at the rear in order to contain new staircases, kitchens, bathrooms and coal storage, and the previously existing two communal privies and two communal washhouses in the yard outside were torn down.

When the Warwickshire Rural Community Council published its review of local charities in June 1973, the boards of Oken's Charity and Eyffler's Charity (mistakenly separated in 1835) had been composed of the same identical sixteen Trustees since 1956, and they had in fact been holding joint meetings for a few years. Oken's was far the larger: Eyffler's only had a small income of some £110, whilst Oken's was about £2,600 – though, as previously related, Oken's Trustees would have had much more if they had not 'surrendered' much of their capital to educational uses in the previous century, and that not to the education of the poor.

By good management, however, the Trustees continued to increase the value of Oken's Charity. The net proceeds of selling Stud Farm land off the Myton Road for building purposes in July 1982 amounted to £132,895, and this was one of the factors responsible for raising the net worth of the Charity in property and investments from £370,000 in November 1980 to £737,841 in June 1985.

*George Tibbits, authority on Oken, holding an item of Oken's silver*

# — 15 —

# *Today*

By a Scheme of July 18th 1988 the two charities of Oken and Eyffler were amalgamated into one body as the Charity of Thomas Oken and Nicholas Eyffler. This is the Scheme by which the Charity operates today with one amendment: it was widened in 1990 so that almshouse applicants are not confined to Warwick residents but can be poor persons "who are either residents or former residents of the Town of Warwick or who have a long-standing association with that town", thereby allowing people living in the immediate rural areas to be eligible also.

The 1988 Scheme reduced the Trustees to the present thirteen, namely the Mayor ex-officio; four Nominated Trustees, one appointed by the District Council and three by the Town Council, to serve for four years, who "may be but need not be members of the appointing council"; and eight Co-opted Trustees serving for five years who "shall be persons who through residence, occupation or employment, or otherwise have special knowledge of the Town of Warwick.".

*The Guild Cottages, Bowling Green Street*

The original Trustees under the present Scheme were Councillors Bryn Brewster, Cherrie Chandley, Gerald Guest, Leo Howlett and Bridget Savory, and Messrs. Leslie Aldington, Jack Butler, Donald Fuller, Robert MacMillan, Patrick Martin, James Pritchard, Ralph Thornton and Herbert Walden, with Terence Horn as Clerk and Receiver.

It was as a united body that the Charity was to build its first new almshouses for three hundred years. Various sites for building or conversion were considered. Among them were the closed United Reformed church in Brook Street, the College Garden adjacent to St. Mary's, and a site in Priory Road where Garden Cottage would have made an ideal warden's home but which was subsequently developed as retirement homes by another body. Eventually a derelict site in Bowling Green Street belonging to the Lord Leycester Hospital which in its time had served both as an air-raid shelter and allotments was acquired in May 1987 for £41,848. Here adjacent to the Hospital and beneath the Wall

*Herbert Walden hands over the Chairmanship of the Trustees to Thomas Bellamy*

which marked the boundary of the mediaeval town seven brand new almshouses were built during 1991. Unlike the single occupancies at Castle Hill these were designed for married couples. The architect was John Danzelman and the tender of Messrs. Willholme Ltd. of Stratford costing £280,583 was accepted. However, the Charity's finances were helped with a grant of £100,000 from King Henry VIII Charity, another of £40,000 from Baron Davenport's Charity, and smaller grants from the Parish of Warwick and other donors. The Guild Cottages, as they were to be officially called, were opened on March 17th 1992 by Lady Benson, the Chairman of the Almshouse Association. The inscription on the front of the buildings reads:

## The Guild Cottages

These almshouses were built by
The Charity of Thomas Oken and Nicholas Eyffler
founded in 1571.
Thomas Oken was the last Master of The Guild
of the Holy Trinity and St. George and a
great benefactor to Warwick
A.D. 1992

The cottages form a pleasant L-shaped courtyard below the walls, and consist of three downstairs flats, three upstairs flats and a bungalow. On the courtyard wall is a brass plaque:

THE GUILD COTTAGES
Built by The Charity of Thomas Oken and Nicholas Eyffler
with financial assistance from
King Henry VIII Charity, Warwick
Baron Davenport's Charity
and the
Parish of Warwick
were officially opened by
LADY BENSON, O.B.E., J.P.
on the 17th March, 1992

| R. H. THORNTON | T. F. HORN |
| --- | --- |
| Chairman of Trustees | Clerk and Receiver |

Architects: Donald James & Partners

No sooner were the new residents settled in than part of the Town Wall immediately behind collapsed and had to be shored up with ugly scaffolding pending repair. But who was to be responsible for that repair? Certainly not Oken's Charity, nor the Lord Leycester Hospital – it was generally believed that Warwick District Council were the owners as successors in 1974 to the assets of the old Borough Council. However, the Council claimed to have evidence they were not the owners – the discovery of Latin documents was mentioned at one stage – but they never produced anything and threatened legal action instead. The Charity had accepted an obligation to maintain the Wall when they acquired the land from the Lord Leycester Hospital, but for maintenance only as against putting the Wall in good condition which was the owner's responsibility. Meanwhile the shoring up of the Wall was a permanent nuisance and inconvenience, if not outright danger, to the residents whilst the negotiations proceeded.

Finally, the dispute was resolved by ignoring the question of ownership and dividing the estimated cost of £109,000 between the three parties concerned, with the Council agreeing to fund any excess. The Charity, therefore, made an immediate ex-gratia payment of £25,000 without prejudice, to be followed by further instalments totalling £11,330. And so, some five years late, the repairs to the Wall were finally completed in 1998.

The next task of the Charity was to refurbish completely the ten single home Castle Hill cottages, all occupied by ladies – though both they and the Trustees were quite happy to have men! The work included the construction of new kitchens and bathrooms. It cost about £300,000, and with £200,000 coming from grants, the Charity drew £100,000 from reserves. The almshouses were officially re-opened on July 29th 1994 by Viscount Daventry, the Lord Lieutenant of the County.

*Castle Hill Almshouses today*

*St. Mary's today viewed from the alley way at the side of Oken's House
(Gordon Flanagan)*

A problem with damp unfortunately continued for some time afterwards, "the ladies suffering with enormous fortitude" (according to the Minutes of the Charity) after already having had to go through relocation during the alterations. Fortunately, the problem turned out to be not nearly as great as the Environmental Health Department of the District Council believed, and it was eventually solved. Indeed the Charity received a Warwick Society Award for the Castle Hill refurbishment. But no sooner had the damp been dealt with than the Trustees had another wall to attend to: in December 1997 the Wall on which the Castle Hill almshouses stood also collapsed! The Trustees naturally saw to it that the wall was promptly repaired and footed a bill for £10,000. They then sought to reclaim the cost from Warwickshire County Council who were thought to be the owners as the successors to the Highway Authority of the day when the road level was reduced and the wall built. But the County Council denied responsibility, and research is still continuing to establish ownership. How ironic that the Charity should be hit twice by wall collapses for which no public body was prepared to take responsibility! Thomas Oken, with his concern for the upkeep of roads and pavements, must be turning in his grave!

One Oken tenant became a centenarian. Ada Thumwood, who had been a resident at No. 1 Castle Hill since 1963, celebrated her 100th birthday on August 21st 1993. The Clerk ensured that she received the Queen's telegram. Unfortunately Mrs. Thumwood had had to go into a nursing home three months previously and she died later in the year. Before moving to Castle Hill she had lived in Castle Street in the shadow of Oken's House.

Terence Horn ceased to be Clerk and Receiver of the Charity at the end of December 2000: during his term of office the charitable activities, assets and income of the Charity had expanded substantially. With thirty-two years of devoted service he is believed to have been the longest serving Clerk in the Charity's history.

# — 16 —

# *How the Charity works*

The thirteen Trustees meet four times a year and the objects of the Charity are (a) the provision and maintenance of almshouses for poor residents who are either former Warwickians or associates of the town of Warwick and (b) the relief of need in general in the event of a surplus. Three permanent sub-committees – the Almshouses Sub-Committee, the Investment and Finance Sub-Committee, and the Feast SubCommittee – meet as required, as do ad hoc sub-committees from time to time, e.g. there was a Castle Hill Baptist Church Redevelopment Sub-Committee meeting when the new Baptist Church was being built next door to the Castle Hill almshouses. The present Trustees' Clerk and Receiver is Mr. Christopher Houghton who was appointed in September 2001. The Clerk advises on legal matters, and the Charity also retains Auditors, Bankers, Architects, an Investment Adviser and a Chartered Surveyor.

The financial activities of the Charity are considered under four headings by the Trustees: a General Fund for routine maintenance and administration; Designated Funds for particular purposes which are transferred back to the General Fund when the purpose has been completed, Restricted Funds where donations are received for a specific use, e.g for the almshouses or cottages, and the Permanent Endowment represented in the value of properties and investments.

Besides Oken's House and the two sets of almshouses, Oken's Charity until recently also owned Stud Farmhouse and garden off the Myton Road and 19 acres of agricultural land there. But when Tom Davies left after renting the house for 60 years and farming the land for most of that time, planning permission was obtained and the farmhouse and garden were sold at auction in June 2000 for a combined figure of £359,000. After deduction of expenses and certain figures for allowances, the Charity's assets increased as a result by something in excess of £200,000. The net proceeds of sale represented Permanent Endowment of the Charity and investments were increased accordingly

The Castle Hill Almshouses are currently (December 31st, 2001) valued at £430,000 and the Guild Cottages at £406,000 (The valuation of Oken's House is presently £143,000, but it has been leased to the County Council since January 1988). The valuations of the two sets of almshouses mean tangible fixed assets of £836,000. Fixed asset investments total £486,086 and current assets in a charities deposit fund, which include monies from the recent sale already mentioned, amount to £433,691. Allowing for liabilities, this means that the total worth of Oken's Charity is currently £1,708,742.

The present Trustees (in December 2002) are the Mayor ex-officio, Councillor Margaret Affleck; four nominated Trustees, Councillors Leslie Caborn, Joan Cooper and Agnes Leddy and Mr. William Renton; and seven co-opted Trustees, Messrs. Thomas Bellamy (Chairman), Terence Brown, David Guest, Donald Hanson, Robert MacMillan and Ralph Thornton and Dr. Ann Thurley. Mr. Herbert Walden had been a Trustee for over thirty years at the time of his death in October 2002.

Today the Trustees continue to run the finances of the Charity prudently, and seek to help others with care and compassion as Thomas Oken himself would have wished.

*A Group of Trustees*

# — 17 —

# *The Legacy of Thomas Oken lives on*

George Tibbits was Clerk and Receiver from 1949 until his untimely death in 1968. During those years there was a great improvement in the fortunes of the Charity, and he was responsible for increasing its annual income from £420 to £1,800, for a very considerable increase in capital funds, and, above all, for the reintroduction of the Feast. He lived and breathed Oken and his lengthy toast to the pious memory which precedes the loyal toast at these dinners was listened to with increasing impatience by those of his hearers who were gasping for a cigarette! But his authoritative treatise on the man and the Charity (unfortunately never published) contains information and conclusions which no one would question without good reason. He was fond of saying that "tradition is the accumulated wisdom of the ages", and nowhere is this more true than in the story of this Charity.

"Ye have ye poor with you always" – as much today as in Oken's time. We rightly no longer patronise them as in the old days when condescension was considered a virtue; we no longer use such an obnoxious term as 'the poor'; and being poor today takes different forms from the past; but the spirit of Oken's epitaph still holds good, and the Trustees continue to follow in his footsteps to ensure that those who need help are indeed helped.

The main concern of the Trustees today is the welfare of the residents of the Castle Hill dwellings and the Guild Cottages, most of whom are neither poor nor aged in the accepted sense of the word. The seven families of retired couples, widows and widowers who live at the Guild Cottages are all over 65, but the lower age of 50 has been retained so that Castle Hill residents, who would have been considered aged in times gone by, can be quite youthful! Five of the seventeen households run cars, an indication of neither extreme poverty nor advanced years! But all of them have been chosen because of their need for somewhere to live.

All of the accommodation at Castle Hill is more or less identical in each flat: bed-sitting room, kitchen and bathroom, with Trust maintained garden at the rear. Approach is from three outside doors giving access to five odd-numbered flats downstairs and five even-numbered above. Separate staircases inside ensure that all ten flats have their own internal front doors, with the lower flats having their own back doors also. 'Bed-sitting room' is really a misnomer, because this living room is remarkably spacious and being L-shaped to a greater or lesser degree it allows the bed to be unobtrusive when you gather round the fire or television. The properties are unfurnished apart from carpets, enabling new residents to bring as much of their own furniture and personal possessions as possible, and the kitchens are as large as in standard three-bedroomed houses. Secondary glazing has just been installed to minimise the noise of traffic outside (double glazing itself is not permitted in such listed buildings), and the gas-fired central heating makes for a cosy atmosphere. Residents pay for their own running expenses – electricity, gas, telephone, council tax – but the cost of decoration and repairs is borne by the Trustees. Each property is fitted with a helpline facility. Mrs. Jill Betts, the previous Clerk's Secretary, was a frequent visitor attentive to their needs for many years, and today Dr. Ann Thurley and other members of the Almshouses Sub-Committee often call. All the residents speak very highly of the care they receive.

Much the same can be said of the Guild Cottages*, though here the spaciousness of the flats in such an apparently confined space is even more remarkable. In addition to kitchen, bathroom and plenty of storage space, there is a separate living room and bedroom, and the latter can accommodate a king-size bed! Double glazing is, of course, standard in such new properties and, unlike the Castle Hill almshouses, each cottage is quite different. For example, one flat has a slightly smaller kitchen than another, but in compensation has a cubby-hole large enough to house a small bureau and a photocopier! In some cases the kitchen is in effect the dining-room, in others it is the sitting-room which serves that purpose. The courtyard at the rear is partly lawn and partly vegetable and flower garden. Although these cottages are designed for couples, if one of them should die the other may continue to live there.

Today residents pay a Weekly Maintenance Contribution (not rent) of £48 per week for the Guild Cottages and £32 at Castle Hill, and housing benefit is available where necessary. Gone are the days of 'objects of charity' – the Trustees visit the residents as friends rather than as landlords – and each year each individual currently gets a Christmas present of £25. And on April 30th 1996 the Trustees invited all the residents to lunch in the Great Hall of the Lord Leycester Hospital in connection with the 425th Anniversary of the foundation of the Charity, and a similar lunch was held on May 3rd 2000 to celebrate the Millennium.

---

\* Other charities manage the three neighbouring sets of 'almshouses' – the Lord Leycester Hospital, Westgate Cottages and Tibbit's Court, named after George Tibbits.

In considering the legacy of Warwick's most famous son, we must also mention the King Henry VIII Charity and Warwick School. There would be no King Henry VIII Charity dispensing monies to organisations in Warwick today if Oken had not so skilfully recovered Guild and Church property from the King's Commissioners all those years ago. And Warwick School would have become extinct if he had not given the boys refuge in his Guildhall when Henry made them homeless – and the school would also have been in considerable difficulty if Oken's Trustees had not come to the rescue so generously – to their own disadvantage – over three centuries later.

No doubt Thomas Oken would be pleasantly surprised by all the work continuing today which stems from his efforts. His spirit lives on, especially to the benefit of many generations of Warwick citizens.

# Bibliography

CAMPBELL, Brabazon – Report on the Charities of the Borough of Warwick (1890)

DUGDALE, Sir William – The Antiquities of Warwickshire (2nd ed. 1730)

FARR, Michael, ed. – The Great Fire of Warwick, 1694 (Dugdale Society, 1992)

FARR, Michael, ed. – Nicholas Eyffeler of Warwick, Glazier (in Dugdale Society Transactions, Vol.31, Miscellany I, 1977)

FIELD, Jean – Kings of Warwick (Brewin Books, 1995)

FIELD, William – An Historical and Descriptive Account of the Town and Castle of Warwick (H. Sharpe, 1815)

FISHER, John – The Black Book of Warwick (ed. by Thomas Kemp, pub. by Henry T. Cooke and Son, 1898)

KEMP, Thomas – A History of Warwick and Its People (Henry T. Cooke and Son, 1905)

KEMP, Thomas – Thomas Oken of Warwick, Mercer (Warwickshire Naturalists' and Archaeologists' Field Club, 1894)

KEMP, Thomas – The Carrying out of the Will of Thomas Oken (Warwickshire Naturalists' and Archaeologists' Field Cliub, 1896)

LEACH, A. F. – History of Warwick School (Constable, 1906)

Lord Leycester Hospital, Warwick (Colourmaster Ltd.)

MORLEY, W. H. – Review of Local Charities for the Poor and the Sick undertaken by Warwickshire Rural Community Council on behalf of the Borough Council of Warwick (June 1973)

Report of His Majesty's Commissioners for Inquiring into the Public Charities of the Borough of Warwick, August 1826 (E. Heathcote, 1830)

RUDD, Julian – Oken's Sermons, 1971 to 1984 (typescript, Oken's Charity, 1984)

TIBBITS, E. George – Ancient Records of Warwick (Dugdale Society Occasional Paper, No.5, 1938)

TIBBITS, E. George – The History of King Henry VIII Charity (typescript)

TIBBITS, E. George – The History of Oken's Charity (typescript, 1968)

TIBBITS, E. George – Miscellaneous manuscript and typescript notes on Oken's Charity (CR1185, Box 3)

The Town Maps of Warwick, 1620 – 1851: an Archive Teaching Unit prepared by the Warwick County Record Office and published by the County Museum.

Victoria History of the County of Warwick, Vol.VIII (O.U.P., 1969)

WALDEN, Herbert – Thomas Oken, St. Mary's and King Henry VIII Charity (typescript, 1998)

WALLIS, Shirley – Thomas Oken: St. Mary's Church and a Remarkable Parishioner (2000)

WALLIS, Shirley, and KUENZLER, Pat – Thomas Oken Then and Now! (typescript, 1993)

(Shirley Wallis has also invented a board game similar to Monopoly based upon the Will of Thomas Oken in which the object is to give away wealth rather than to accumulate it)

WILSON, Philip – The History of Thomas Oken (typescript, 1963)

For a list of the Charity's documents deposited at the County Record Office see their Warwick Charities Union Catalogue, Vol. 2, pp.1 – 14: Thomas Oken's Charity

Reference has also been made to 16th century College and Corporation accounts.

# *Index*